THE
GREATEST LEADER
WHO WASN'T

A Leadership Fable by Charles Manz

Illustrated by Jeevan Sivasubramaniam

The  Company

Helping organizations achieve success through Ethical
Leadership and Values-Based Business Practices

To order additional copies of this book, or for information
on other WALK THE TALK® products and services,
contact us at
1.888.822.9255
or visit our website at
www.walkthetalk.com

THE GREATEST LEADER WHO WASN'T

The key lessons of this poetic fable are based on a practical leadership model that
Charles Manz developed with his colleague and co-author Henry Sims, Jr. A more
extensive description of this model can be found in their book *The New SuperLeadership:
Leading Others to Lead Themselves*, (Berrett-Koehler, 2001).

ISBN 1-885228-63-5

Printed in the United States of America
10 9 8 7 6 5 4 3 2 1

Produced and edited by Steve Ventura
Printed by MultiAd

CONTENTS

NTRODUCTION

Have you ever wrestled with the challenges of being a leader? Have you ever struggled to find the right leadership approach when you have been in charge of someone else, a group, or of a project of some kind? If you've ever been "in charge" – even for only a brief time – at work, in your community, in your family, on a sports team, or in any of the various other aspects of your life, this book is for you!

In a moment, you will begin reading a fable. It tells the story of a man struggling to find a leadership approach that works for him and those he leads. It suggests some different ways of leading ... and their potential consequences. While there are literally hundreds of management theories, this story captures perhaps the most prevalent alternatives to the actual practice of leadership.

The fable is intentionally written in a lighthearted, rhyming style similar to that used by Dr. Seuss. I hope you enjoy the story and have fun with it. More importantly, I hope you realize that it has some very important lessons to remember and apply. You will find that there is much to be learned from one person's quest to find the ingredients of successful leadership in the face of some very significant challenges.

As the story unfolds, the leader of a struggling company with great potential tries several leadership approaches – all in an attempt to get his employees to do what he wants and thinks should be done.

Four primary leader types are introduced during this quest:

- An *autocratic* leader who gains compliance from others through fear and intimidation;

- A *reward-focused* leader who exchanges incentives for follower compliance;

- A *visionary, inspirational* leader who promotes follower commitment to his cause; and finally ...

- A strikingly new kind of leader – one who *leads others to be their own leaders.*

You will see how employees respond to these different leadership approaches. Sometimes, their responses seem quite positive – at least in the short run. But you'll see that many unintended and undesirable side effects also surface.

Eventually, the leader receives a profound message from an employee – one that prompts him to redefine what leadership means ... for him *and* his workforce. Ultimately, he creates an entire company of leaders who exude creativity, solve problems, demonstrate initiative, take responsibility, and lead the organization into a positive turn around, together.

Enjoy this story and think deeply about its implications for you and those with whom you interact. I wish you much personal success as you learn the powerful secrets of being The Greatest Leader Who Wasn't.

THE FABLE

Once upon a time ...

*T*here was a grand company.

It was far far away,

in a thick corporate jungle

that hummed

night and day.

The company did work

on a thing called "the web."

It didn't make hard things,

it made SOFTware instead.

It sold other companies

vast boxes of goods

that helped their computers

to do what they should.

Big things they had planned

for the next corporate line.

New e-ware bells and whistles

that truly were fine.

The products brought

musical whirlwinds,

and even made rain.

They flashed lightening

and thunder,

and cured lower back pain.

They balanced nutrition

with cake and pizza pies.

And built physical fitness

without need for exercise.

No need to exert effort

or be on the ball.

For this line of e-products

alone did it all.

At least that's the claim

this organization did make.

"The best of all products" ...

a miracle for Pete's sake.

The company was led

by a leader

thought so grand.

The earth seemed

to tremble

wherever he would stand.

And the workers all knew

their place underneath

the leader's small entourage –

the executives of grief.

The leader called a meeting,

to speak to his vast troops.

 A time to

remind them all

of their

worker-jump-through hoops.

With self-important majesty,

the leader rose up high.

He looked right through his people

with a gleam upon his eye.

"I am the one who knows," he said

in his forceful leader voice.

"My mighty profile shows," he thought.

"For me they should rejoice!"

"As a leader who's so grand,

I could lead them right through hell.

I'd take them past

the stars so high,

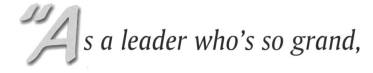

to an astro-victory bell!"

"I do not have a single doubt,

without me they would fall.

I am so great that they'd be lost –

All hope would leave the hall."

*T*hen someone coughed "ahem," and burst the dream that he did see –

A dream of greatness he believed was his rightful destiny.

"*Oh yes, um, follow me,*" *said he*

in his commanding leader voice.

"*Do strictly as I say,*" *he barked,*

"*for you there is no choice.*"

But as time passed,

good products never lined

the warehouse shelves.

The people failed to hit the mark —

they just embarrassed themselves.

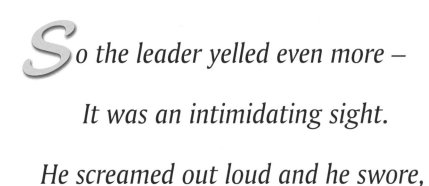

So the leader yelled even more –

It was an intimidating sight.

He screamed out loud and he swore,

with great bark

and equal bite.

*S*cores of workers he did fire.

Many more were

punished and blamed.

But the lack

of progress

continued on.

The workers could not be tamed.

The he workers feared his visciousness

and what he'd do should they fail.

They viewed him not as a great king,

but as a beast with a beastly tail.

*O*h what a tyrant he was then.

Scary muscles he did flex.

The workers saw themselves the prey,

for this man they called BOSS-REX.

There was little creativity.

People had no ideas of their own.

Their only thoughts were

what the leader yelled

through his loud e-magaphone.

These yes men and yes women

tried to read the leader's mind.

They sought to do just as he wished,

despite choices of a better kind.

Then one day,

the leader surmised:

"I'm not getting the results I seek.

Perhaps my style of leadership

is making people meek."

So to change his whole approach

new ideas he did scheme.

"I know – I'll use rewards instead,

to manipulate my team."

He held up grand incentives bright

of gold and options too –

for the workers' strict compliance

in all that they would do.

He patted backs and offered praise.

Smiles to all faces came.

"Is this the leader we have had?

He's clearly not the same."

This was a whole

new kind of boss –

granting wishes large and teeny.

By leading with

rewards, instead,

he soon became

BOSS-GENIE.

"Things are so much better now," the boss thought to himself.

"Good products cannot help but fill each empty warehouse shelf."

*B*ut after time he didn't see

new products on the shelves.

The workers were committed –

but only

to themselves.

"Whats's in it for us?"

they began to ask

of the man who was in charge.

"We'll deliver all the goods you want

if our take is very large."

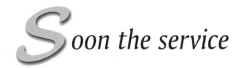

oon the service

to their clients fell.

It was not good – not good at all.

"Don't look at me ...

It's not my job,"

the workers did now call.

They no longer worked in fear.

And they were happier too.

But only that which came with gifts

is all that they would do.

What started out as simple ploys

for all the women and gents,

had truly backfired on the boss —

they became entitlements.

No matter how

the leader tried

to add or change

rewards,

the workers

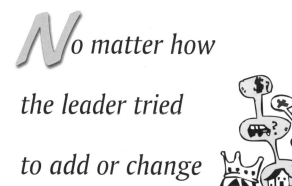

still were much too choosy

in what they would work towards.

So once again he chose to lead

another way instead.

"I'll inspire them with my vision,

and all my charisma," he said.

Most grandly did he stroll,

right to the center stage.

And he looked at the horizon

with an all-so-knowing gaze.

"First we'll capture

the bright moon,

and then the flaming sun.

We will own the entire universe

by the time that we are done!"

"So gather all together now.

And then, come follow me.

I can lead you to a glorious

and spectacular victory."

"You're by far the greatest workers

in the universe you see.

And why not – with such a leader

as smart and grand as me?!"

*H*e marched about

with chest pushed out,

his head held way up high.

And all the while he strained to get

a gleam upon his eye.

He declared himself a hero,

and claimed great vision, too.

By exuding such charisma,

he was labeled BOSS-GURU.

Oh what lofty inspiration

his leadership did make.

The workers would do anything —

whatever it would take.

They followed his great vision,

wherever he would go.

As long as he remained nearby

the workers would still glow.

He issued proclamations,

and exhorted much great work.

The people followed his vision –

every nuance

and small quirk.

But all too soon the visionary

learned he did not know it all.

He could not make all decisions.

He could not call every call.

Although the company

had experts –

some from far and some from near,

they just stood there in a trance

waiting for the leader to steer.

*W*hen he asked for their advice,

they all said, "We know YOU know.

You're the greatest leader ever.

We will follow where you go."

When the leader had to travel

and see to other things,

the workers all just

shrugged and formed

into chaotic rings.

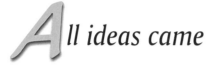ll ideas came

from the leader.

No one else had thoughts at all.

So once again the company hit

a huge, gigantic wall.

ike enthusiastic sheep

they roamed —

wherever the leader'd lead.

If he barely hinted at any turn,

that's the way

they would stampede.

"This is no good either,"

said the leader oh so low.

"We need to go to places

that I don't even know."

Just then,

a sharp young worker

in a small and tiny voice,

said "We could do much better,

if you gave us all a choice."

She slipped a piece of paper into the leader's shaky hand.

He read it with surprise, and began to understand.

So the leader changed his tune.

He began to let it show

that he needed all the workers' help,

to go where they should go.

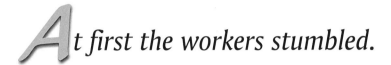

At first the workers stumbled.

From problems they did shrink.

They'd all become dependent

on what the leader'd think.

*B*ut he started asking questions,

and gave up on commands.

He encouraged all the workers

to form in little bands.

*H*e implemented training then

on how to work alone –

and how to work together, too.

Their talents they did hone.

He shared lots of information.

He told them all he knew.

There were

no longer secrets.

He trusted all his crew.

He gave them lots of power

to decide on what to do ...

and provided gobs of input,

at the top

and bottom, too.

He encouraged every worker.

He empowered everyone –

so that all could give their best

and now their own jobs run.

He toned down his own ego

in nearly every case.

He humbly led from behind –

freeing talent in the workplace.

*S*ome called him SuperLeader.

With the strength of all he led.

Rather than taking charge himself

he shared leadership instead.

Soon decisions were being made

by those who really knew.

Expertise, innovation,

and the firm itself,

ALL really grew.

Everyone became a leader.

At least of their own self.

They offered all their know-how

to put products on the shelf.

The many teams of workers

put the firm back on the mend.

They became so strong and able,

on them you could depend.

*A*nd then finally it happened.

The warehouse shelves were filled!!

They overflowed with products,

that they themselves did build.

"We did it!" the workers cried
with a loud and pride-filled cheer.
"We did it by ourselves,
and we did it all right here."

The SuperLeader smiled,

and though receiving no acclaim,

he none-the-less was proud

and very happy

just the same.

So, what's the profound lesson?

Why'd the leader share command?

What was written on the paper

that was in the leader's hand?

*H*e had opened up the paper

and found new hope

as he read

the words of a

very wise man –

from ancient China, it is said ...

Leaders are the best

when you barely know they're around.

They are at their absolute best

when they scarce make any sound.

They are not very good

when obeyed and acclaimed.

But they're even worse

with workers hostilely tamed.

But when leaders are good,

not just good but the best,

they rely not on *their* strength

but on the strength of the rest.

When all the work is done
there will be so much well-earned pride,

that the workers will all say,

"The very best are on our side."

And when the leader's done

(and helped them fill the shelves)

the workers say out loud,

"We did it all ourselves!"

The End

MEET THE LEADERS FROM THE FABLE

Imagine for a moment that you are the leader in the story. Your work force is currently unmotivated and uncommitted, and your high-potential company seems to be stagnating. What style of leadership would you use?

The Greatest Leader Who Wasn't introduces four of the most common approaches to leadership. Each can generate influence and create favorable results – at least in the short run. But, unintended side effects and long-term problems can result from several of the styles, as well.

The first leadership style portrayed in the story is that of "Boss-Rex" – a person who uses a direct, controlling approach. Meanwhile, "Boss-Genie" focuses on using the carrot (rewards) and sometimes the stick. Both of these leaders generate employee compliance ... and not much else. The "Boss-Guru," on the other hand, can foster "above and beyond the call of duty" commitment – based on the leader's inspiration and vision. Nevertheless, all three approaches are *leader centered.* They can create follower dependence and impair people's capacity for self-leadership.

In the end, we see that it's the "SuperLeader" who encourages independence, teamwork, and a deep sense of ownership and purpose. The SuperLeader leads others to lead themselves.

"Boss-Rex"

A controlling, punitive, intimidating leader who typically gets short-term results (which can be handy in a crisis) but creates dependence and longer-term problems.

The Boss-Rex produces followers who are:

- motivated by fear.

- unoriginal and uncreative thinkers.

- compliant but not committed.

- "yes people" driven by the question,
  How can I stay out of trouble with the boss?

"Boss-Genie"

An incentive-focused leader who, by using rewards much like bribes, is able to get gradual results over the longer run (which can be helpful for narrowly-targeted behaviors when there is not a crisis) but creates dependency.

The Boss-Genie produces followers who are:

- motivated by greed and self-interest.

- preoccupied with "playing the game" in order to receive more rewards.

- compliant (as long as the rewards keep coming) but not committed.

- "transactors" driven by the question, *What's in it for me?*

"Boss-Guru"

Focused on inspiration, vision, and charisma, this leader is able to achieve both short and long-term results by inspiring others (which can be helpful when faced with major change or crisis – and when it is important that followers go above and beyond the call of duty) but also creates dependency.

The Boss-Guru produces followers who are:

- motivated by the leader's vision.

- passionate about their work as long as the leader stays around and provides inspiration.

- committed to the leader and his or her cause.

- "enthusiastic sheep" who are often lost if the leader is no longer around.

"SuperLeader"

Instead of being "all powerful," this is an EMPOWERING leader who: 1) leads others to lead themselves; 2) achieves long-term, sustainable results by tapping the leadership potential of every person; 3) enables followers to address, fix, and prevent problems whether or not the leader is around; 4) fosters independence and *inter*dependence.

The SuperLeader produces followers who are:

- internally motivated and believe in themselves.

- deeply committed with psychological ownership.

- independent and interdependent thinkers who pursue continuous improvement.

- "self-leaders" who no longer are mere followers.

*B*ECOMING A SUPERLEADER

Now that you've read the *The Greatest Leader Who Wasn't,* you may have some questions such as: How can I apply these lessons in meeting my own leadership challenges? What can I do to adopt the style and characteristics of a SuperLeader? The following material offers a place to start:

BECOME AN EFFECTIVE SELF-LEADER. Look in the mirror and lead yourself first. Set challenging but achievable goals and reward yourself when you accomplish them. Redesign your job so that you find it more motivating – while still meeting all of your responsibilities. Practice thinking constructively and positively so that you take advantage of opportunities rather than retreating from obstacles.

MODEL SELF-LEADERSHIP FOR YOUR TEAM MEMBERS. Once you've mastered some self-leadership strategies yourself, vividly display these techniques so your followers can learn from them. Demonstrate self-leadership behaviors in a clear and credible manner – giving followers a chance to try them out and adapt them to their own needs.

ENCOURAGE FOLLOWERS TO SET THEIR OWN GOALS. Personal goal setting is so important that it deserves special attention. Help followers understand the importance of identifying challenging but realistic targets for their performance. Guide them in the beginning, then gradually allow them to take over the process.

CREATE POSITIVE THOUGHT PATTERNS. Help followers to see their own potential and capabilities ... and to believe in themselves. Also, encourage them to look for the opportunities nested in problems – rather than focusing on all the reasons to give up and stop trying.

REWARD SELF-LEADERSHIP and PROMOTE CONSTRUCTIVE FEEDBACK. Recognize followers for showing initiative, taking on responsibility, and demonstrating self-leadership rather than merely complying with your wishes or requirements. As followers gain confidence, they will be better able to accept critical feedback on how they can improve – as long as that feedback is constructive in nature. Over time, they will develop the ability to provide that same type of feedback to themselves and others.

PROMOTE SELF-LED TEAMWORK. Encourage followers to work together and help one another. Teams are crucial for effective worker empowerment. Team members can (and will) encourage and reinforce one another – especially if you set the example.

FOSTER A SELF-LEADING CULTURE. Work to establish values and norms that center on initiative and self-leadership. Encourage problem solving by teaching people how to develop solutions rather than giving the solutions to them. Allow followers as much discretion as they can handle. Turn mistakes into learning opportunities. And get in the habit of saying, "What do YOU think we should do?"

CLOSING THOUGHTS

The fable in this book presents us with an apparent paradox: People need leadership in order to *not* need leadership! SuperLeaders tend to develop followers who – because they become both independent and *inter*dependent – move beyond the need for a leader (in the traditional sense). These so called "followers" become very capable of standing on their own feet as they effectively contribute to the team. Do they make mistakes? Of course! But they learn from those mistakes and therefore are not afraid to take reasonable risks. They take ownership of, and pride in, their work. Eventually, they rise above the concept of follower – becoming effective, empowered, confident, LEADERS in their own right.

Effectively apply the concepts of SuperLeadership and your organization will be able to move beyond the need for a few central pillars of leadership strength. Instead, it will be supported by countless pillars – the many capable self-leaders who have the confidence and authority to take initiative and responsibility without always having to look to you – the designated leader – for direction and motivation. Help make that happen and you'll not only benefit your workers and your organization, you'll also enhance your reputation ... and your career.

In the end, the very best label you could possibly earn is:

THE GREATEST LEADER ... WHO WASN'T.

HE AUTHOR

Charles C. Manz, Ph.D., is a speaker, consultant, and best-selling business author. He was a Marvin Bower Fellow at the Harvard Business School and currently holds the Charles and Janet Nirenberg Chair of Business Leadership in the Isenberg School of Management at the University of Massachusetts. His work has been featured on radio, television, and in scores of publications such as *The Wall Street Journal, Fortune, U.S. News & World Report, Success, Psychology Today,* and *Fast Company*.

Dr. Manz has served as a consultant for many organizations, including: 3M, Ford, Motorola, Xerox, the Mayo Clinic, Procter & Gamble, General Motors, American Express, Allied Signal, Unisys, Josten's Learning, Banc One, the American Hospital Association, and both the United States and Canadian governments.

He has authored or co-authored over 100 articles and 17 books, including the bestsellers *Business Without Bosses: How Self-Managing Teams Are Building High-Performing Companies,* the Stybel-Peabody prize winning *SuperLeadership: Leading Others to Lead Themselves,* and *The Leadership Wisdom of Jesus: Practical Lessons For Today.* His newest works are *Fit to Lead: The Proven 8-Week Solution for Shaping Up Your Body, Your Mind, and Your Career,* and *Temporary Sanity: Instant Self-Leadership Strategies for Turbulent Times.*

*T*HE ILLUSTRATOR

Jeevan Sivasubramaniam is the senior managing editor at Berrett-Koehler Publishers. He is not a professional illustrator by any stretch of the imagination, but is thankful for opportunities to exercise his doodling skills. He lives in San Francisco with his wife and cat, and spends his spare time teaching people how to pronounce his last name.

WALK THE TALK®
PRESENTATIONS & WORKSHOPS

Bring Charles Manz and his powerful leadership messages to your organization. Favorite presentations of his clients include:

- *The New SuperLeadership*
- *Emotional Discipline*
- *The Power of Failure*
- *Mastering Self Leadership*
- *Leading Self-Managed Teams*

WALK THE TALK Presentations and Workshops are customized to your audience, organizational culture, and targeted business objectives. Our cadre of experienced authors and facilitators are dedicated to providing you with a powerful educational experience – and committed to helping ensure the complete success of your sponsored event.

We offer educational programs and presentations on each topic covered in our best selling books to include:

- Effective Leadership Techniques
- Business Ethics and Values Alignment
- Coaching and Performance Improvement Strategies
- Building Customer Service Attitudes and Behaviors
- Techniques to Attract and Retain "The Best and Brightest Employees"
- Building a High-Performance Culture
- Dealing With Organizational Change
  And much, much more!

To learn more:
Call 972.243.8863 or toll free 800.888.2811
Email info@walkthetalk.com

Send me additional copies of THE GREATEST LEADER WHO WASN'T

1-24 copies: $12.95 each   100-499 copies: $10.95 each
25-99 copies: $11.95 each   500+ copies: *Call 1.888.822.9255*

THE GREATEST LEADER WHO WASN'T   ____ copies X _____ = $_____

OTHER LEADERSHIP DEVELOPMENT PRODUCTS

The Leadership Secrets of SANTA CLAUS   ____ copies X $ 12.95 = $_____
WALK THE TALK ... And Get The Results You Want   ____ copies X $ 12.95 = $_____
LEADERSHIP COURAGE   ____ copies X $ 14.95 = $_____
LEADERSHIP DEVELOPMENT LIBRARY   ____ sets X $ 99.95 = $_____

Client Priority Code:
504DB

Product Total	$_____
Shipping & Handling	$_____
Subtotal	$_____

Sales Tax:

(Sales & Use Tax Collected on TX & CA Customers Only)

Texas Sales Tax – 8.25%	$_____
CA Sales/Use Tax	$_____
Total (U.S. Dollars Only)	$_____

Shipping and Handling Charges

No. of Items	1-4	5-9	10-24	25-49	50-99	100-199	200+
Total Shipping	$7.95	$10.95	$17.95	$26.95	$48.95	$84.95	$89.95+$0.25/book

Orders shipped ground delivery 5-7 days. Next and 2nd business day delivery available – call 1.888.822.9255. Call 972.243.8863 for quote if outside continental U.S.

Name_____ Title _____

Organization_____

Shipping Address_____
(No P.O. Boxes)

City_____ State_____ Zip _____

Phone_____ Fax_____

E-Mail_____

Charge Your Order: ☐ MasterCard   ☐ Visa   ☐ American Express

Credit Card Number_____ Exp. Date_____

☐ Check Enclosed (Payable to: The WALK THE TALK Company)

☐ Please Invoice (Orders over $250 ONLY) P. O. Number (if required)_____

PHONE	FAX	
1.888.822.9255	972-243-0815	**MAIL**
or 972.243.8863	**ON-LINE**	WALK THE TALK Co.
M-F, 8:30-5:00 Cen.	www.walkthetalk.com	2925 LBJ Fwy., #201
		Dallas, TX 75234

Prices effective February 2005 are subject to change.